Etna Elementary
107590 U.S. 89 Nth.
Etna, WY 83118
307-885-2472

Phil Wilson 10-6-95

Published by Smart Apple Media
1980 Lookout Drive, North Mankato, Minnesota 56003
Produced by Byron Preiss Visual Publications, Inc.

Cover design by Dean Motter
Interior design by Gilda Hannah
Edited by Howard Zimmerman

Front cover art by Phil Wilson
Back cover art by Jan Sovak

Art Credits: Pages 1, 5, 9 © 2002 Phil Wilson. Page 2 © 2002 Joe Tucciarone.
Page 7 © 2002 Patrick O'Brien. Page 11 © 2002 Jan Sovak. Page 13 © 2002 Christopher
Srnka. Page 15 © 2002 Rich Penney. Pages 16–17, 19, 25 © 2002 Gregory S. Paul.
Page 17 (inset) © 2002 Berislav Krzic. Page 21 © 2002 John Sibbick. Page 23 © 2002
Kelly Taylor. Page 27 © 2002 Karen Carr. Pages 28–29 © 2002 Douglas Henderson.
Pages 30–31 © 2002 Daniel Varner.

Printed in the U.S.A.

Library of Congress Cataloging-in-Publication Data

Olshevsky, George.
Diplodocus / by George Olshevsky and Sandy Fritz.
p. cm.—(Discovering dinosaurs)
Summary: Presents information on *Diplodocus*, including physical
characteristics, diet, habitat, known social organization, close relatives, and areas where
fossils have been found.
ISBN 1-58340-177-6
1. Diplodocus—Juvenile literature. [1. Diplodocus. 2. Dinosaurs.]
I. Fritz, Sandy. II. Title.
QE862.S3 O458 2002
567.913—dc21   2002017632

First Edition

2 4 6 8 9 7 5 3 1

DIPLODOCUS

Sandy Fritz and George Olshevsky

SMART APPLE MEDIA

inosaurs lived on Earth from about 227 million to 65 million years ago. Scientists call this the Mesozoic era. It is also called the Age of Reptiles or the Age of Dinosaurs. Dinosaurs were closely related to today's reptiles and birds. In fact, many scientists now think that birds evolved from a small meat-eating dinosaur that was a swift runner. All dinosaurs were land animals. Flying reptiles (called pterosaurs) and reptiles that swam in the sea also lived during this period, but they were not dinosaurs.

The Age of Dinosaurs, the Mesozoic era, is divided into three periods. The earliest period is called the Triassic, which lasted from 248 million to 205 million years ago. Dinosaurs first appeared around the middle of this period. The Jurassic period followed, lasting from 205 million to 145 million years ago. The final period is called the Cretaceous. The Cretaceous spanned from 145 million to 65 million years ago. After the Cretaceous, dinosaurs were gone.

But during their time, dinosaurs lived everywhere on Earth, even in Antarctica. About 700 different kinds of dinosaurs have been unearthed, and many more remain in the ground awaiting discovery. There were meat-eating dinosaurs that could run fast on their long hind legs. There were four-legged, plant-eating dinosaurs 150 feet (46 m) long and weighing as much as 100 tons (91 t)! There were dinosaurs with horns, crests, and bony armor. Some dinosaurs, both meat-eaters and plant-eaters, were as small as chickens or house cats.

Everything we know about dinosaurs comes from fossils that people have dug up from the ground. Scientists examine, measure, and analyze these fossils. From them we can learn when and where dinosaurs lived. We have learned how dinosaurs walked and ran, what they hunted, and what plants they ate. We can even figure out how long they lived. Presented in this series is the most up-to-date information we have learned about dinosaurs. We hope you'll enjoy reading all about the fabulous beasts of Earth's distant past.

The Sauropod Family

They were giants in a world of giants. No other dinosaurs grew bigger or heavier or longer than sauropods. These four-legged plant-eaters towered over all other animals. *Diplodocus* belonged to the sauropod family. It stretched 90 feet (27 m), longer than two 18-wheel tractor-trailers placed end-to-end. *Diplodocus* is one of the longest land animals ever found. But in a way, its record-making length is misleading. The dinosaur's body was only 20 feet (6 m) long. The other 70 feet (21 m) was neck and, mostly, tail.

Compared to other sauropods, *Diplodocus* was a lightweight. Some of its cousins were real earth-shakers. *Supersaurus* tipped

> The largest sauropod yet discovered is *Sauroposeidon*. Each of its neck bones was about four feet (1.2 m) long. This giant brachiosaurid was built like a giraffe. But it was 60 feet (18.2 m) tall, and weighed about 60 tons (54.5 t). It may have been the largest land animal that ever lived. The name *Sauroposeidon* means "earthquake god lizard."

An *Allosaurus* tries attacking a young diplodocid.

the scales at more than 50 tons (45 t). *Brachiosaurus* weighed in at around 63 tons (57 t). *Diplodocus* probably weighed only 18 tons (16 t), which is roughly equal to the combined weight of four adult elephants.

Although they varied in size, all sauropods shared similar features. They had a tiny head, a long neck, an elephant-like body, and a long tail. Several groups of sauropods have been discovered. The two main groups are the brachiosaurids and the diplodocids. The brachiosaurids had the shortest tails of all sauropods. Their front legs were as long as, or longer than, their back legs. This gave brachiosaurids an upright stance that let them raise their necks high above the ground. Brachiosaurids were the giraffes of the Jurassic. They became the tallest and heaviest land animals ever to walk the planet.

The diplodocids were very different sauropods. Instead of growing tall like the brachiosaurids, the diplodocids grew long. They had the longest tails of all sauropods. Their hind legs were longer than their front legs. This forward-leaning stance probably favored feeding on plants lower to the ground. Diplodocids were usually much lighter than brachiosaurids. They became the *longest* animals to ever walk the planet.

In Texas, scientists found a fossil trackway left by a sauropod similar to *Diplodocus*. They determined the giant plant-eater was moving at about four miles per hour (6.4 kph). The animal had about the same walking speed as a modern elephant.

Some members of the sauropod group. In the foreground is *Diplodocus*. The three sauropods with tall, giraffe-like necks are brachiosaurids. Diplodocids and brachiosaurids are the two main branches of the sauropod family.

Diplodocus lived in the late Jurassic, roaming the shores of a shallow inland sea that divided North America. During the Jurassic period, the earth looked quite different. No grass grew, and there were no flowers. For the most part, plants and trees that are now extinct dominated the planet.

At the beginning of the Jurassic, the earth's continents were bunched together to form a single, giant landmass. Scientists call this super-continent Pangea. Large areas of inland Pangea were barren and dry. By the end of the Jurassic, some 140 million years ago, Pangea had separated into four continents.

When *Diplodocus* lived, the world was generally warmer. There were no ice caps at the North Pole and South Pole. The atmosphere was full of moisture, and most of the world was bathed in tropical temperatures. Plant life during the Jurassic was widespread and abundant. There was enough plant food to satisfy the appetites of gigantic plant-eating dinosaurs like *Diplodocus*.

Diplodocus Old and New

The discovery of a 90-foot-long (27 m), snake-necked, whip-tailed monster thrilled the public in the 1870s. And yet, the scientists who began to reconstruct the fossil bones had no idea what a dinosaur looked like.

Most early illustrations of *Diplodocus* show an animal that no one would recognize today as a dinosaur. Instead, it looked like a giant crocodile. Most everyone believed *Diplodocus* was a lumpish lizard that walked with its legs bent and its tail dragging on the ground. This dinosaur, they thought, had paddled around in

A *Diplodocus* mother and baby. Sauropod babies had to grow quickly to avoid predators, and to avoid being stepped on by adults.

swamps, eating water plants. But our understanding of *Diplodocus* changed as more and more dinosaur fossils were discovered.

Scientists realized that *Diplodocus* had legs that resembled the legs of an elephant rather than the legs of lizards. With their stout legs held straight beneath them to support their weight, sauropods walked the land like elephants. Fossil footprints, called trackways, suggest that sauropods may have walked great distances on land.

Weight was a problem for a dinosaur as big as *Diplodocus*. One solution to the weight problem is to keep bones as light as possible. For this reason *Diplodocus* had many hollow spaces in its skeleton. Whereas some sauropods had vertebrae, or spinal bones, that were solid, *Diplodocus* had vertebrae that were hollowed out.

Diplodocus's long neck was also designed for lightness. The bones were full of air pockets. This made them far lighter than if they were made of solid bone.

Leg bones were not hollowed out because these bones needed to be especially solid for added strength. The solid leg bones fit directly under the animal's body to help support its massive weight.

Another lightweight feature helped make *Diplodocus* more sturdy. There were strips of bone that were embedded in the skin of the animal's belly. They were loosely attached to the skeleton and probably helped support the animal's inner organs.

The neck bones overlapped, which helped to support the neck, but also limited sideways movement. The long tail helped to balance the weight of the neck and head.

A mother and juvenile *Diplodocus* feed on ferns. Diplodocids probably ate low-lying ferns and plants, and from the lower branches of trees.

Despite its colossal size, *Diplodocus* had a tiny head. At only two feet (.6 m) long, the giant's head was about the size of a modern horse's head. On top of that, *Diplodocus* had a brain the size of a walnut. Scientists still can't explain how a walnut-sized brain could have controlled such a giant animal.

Recent research has changed our view of *Diplodocus's* head. It was once thought that their nostrils were high up on their heads, above the eyes. This made sense when it was believed that *Diplodocus* spent most of its time in water. After all, whales and dolphins have high nostrils so they can snatch a gulp of air without lifting their heads entirely out of the water. But now it seems that sauropods like *Diplodocus* had large, complex nasal cavities. This finding suggests that most sauropods had nostrils at the front of their snouts, like alligators and crocodiles. Now artists must create new illustrations that show this new view of the dinosaur's nostrils.

A young *Allosaurus* makes the mistake of attacking a *Diplodocus*. One strike from the whip-like tail could cripple the predator, leaving it unable to hunt.

Brachiosaurids could move their long necks far above their backs. This allowed them to feed from the upper branches of trees. Diplodocids probably did not hold their heads high in the air, but swept them from side-to-side when feeding.

Opposite page, top: The head of *Diplodocus* shows its peg-like teeth. Above: A pair of meat-eaters run into a herd of sauropods, trying to get at one of the babies.

Diplodocus's Eating Habits

By looking at *Diplodocus*'s teeth, we can discover how and what this dinosaur ate. *Diplodocus*'s skull was narrow and pointed. Its teeth were bunched together like groups of pencils in the front of its mouth. The teeth were used to strip plants and trees of their leaves. *Diplodocus* did not chew its food. Food was swallowed whole. But if *Diplodocus* had no teeth to chew with, how did it break up its food to digest it?

Diplodocus probably had more than one stomach. Once swallowed, food went through a series of stomach chambers, called gizzards, that helped crush and digest the meal. The fossil evidence for gizzards comes from stones called gastroliths. These stones were swallowed, and settled in the gizzards. When the gizzards contracted, stomach acid and the stones helped grind up the food.

Gastroliths have been found with several sauropod fossils. One relative of *Diplodocus* was found with two separate piles of gizzard stones. It is likely that *Diplodocus* also swallowed gizzard stones to help digest its food.

During most of the Jurassic period, grasses and flowering plants did not yet exist. Ferns were common, and came in many forms. Some were small like modern ferns, but some grew to be as big as trees. Soft ferns probably made up part of *Diplodocus*'s diet.

Cycads were another common plant. These look like small, squat palm trees rising about three feet (1 m) off the ground. Growing a bit higher were now-extinct trees called cycadeoids. These trees resembled cycads but were more slender.

Apatosaurus, a heavily
built diplodocid, reaches
for the lower branches
of a conifer tree.

Some scientists think *Diplodocus* may have stood on its back legs to reach high tree branches. This could have placed its head as much as 50 feet (15 m) off the ground, bringing it within range of the lower branches on giant redwood trees.

Conifer trees about 15 to 16 feet (5 m) tall were probably the main source of food for *Diplodocus*. At this height, young pine trees flourished. It's easy to picture an adult *Diplodocus* standing in a grove of young trees, stripping the needles from the branches with its teeth. Without moving its body, it could swing its long neck to feed from other nearby trees.

Friends and Enemies

The late Jurassic world was full of animals that seem gigantic to us. Flying reptiles called pterosaurs flapped through the sky. Some were as big as small airplanes. In the seas, giant marine reptiles such as *Plesiosaurus* and *Mosasaurus* grew as long as 50 to 100 feet (15–30 m). *Diplodocus* also shared its world with other plant-eaters. Armor-plated dinosaurs such as *Stegosaurus* lumbered around in the same part of the world as *Diplodocus*. So did tank-like, armored dinosaurs called ankylosaurs. Mammals also lived during the Jurassic period. Many were small, mouse-like creatures that were active at night.

Allosaurs were perhaps the most feared hunters of the late Jurassic period. They lived all over the world during the late Jurassic. They were extremely successful predators. A full-grown *Allosaurus* could reach 36 feet (11 m) in length, and stood about 16 feet (5 m) high. Yet it was light, weighing only one to two tons (.9–1.8 t).

In the foreground is *Baryonyx*, a strange-looking meat-eater with a skull like a crocodile's. In the distance, a couple of brachiosaurids feed from the top branches of evergreen trees.

These dinosaurs were killing machines. They could run fast and had large heads filled with sharp teeth. Allosaurs may have hunted young *Diplodocus*.

An adult *Diplodocus* had little to fear from predators. The sheer size of a full-grown *Diplodocus* would have acted as a defensive weapon all by itself. Once a prey animal gets too large, predators stay away from it. A plant-eating dinosaur weighing around 10 to 20 tons (11–22 t) would have fed many predators for many days. *Diplodocus* needed to be able to defend itself. But with no visible armor, no protective spikes, and weak teeth, how did *Diplodocus* do it? With its four legs firmly planted, *Diplodocus* could have used its long, whip-like tail as a weapon.

Diplodocus had the longest and most whip-like tail of any sauropod. Other plant-eating dinosaurs used their tails for defense. The spikes on a *Stegosaurus*'s tail were potent weapons. The bony club on an *Ankylosaurus*'s tail could have crushed the bones of an attacker. If these dinosaurs used their tails for defense, why couldn't *Diplodocus*? Scientists think that when alarmed or under attack, it's possible that *Diplodocus* used its tail like a whip, cracking and snapping it in defense.

Ceratosaurus was another predator in the late Jurassic. It was about the size of an Allosaurus. Here it is trying to attack the armored plant-eater Stegosaurus, but it had better be wary of those tail spikes.

Diplodocus's Behavior

Fossil bones can reveal what an animal looked like, how it stood, and even how much it weighed. Some fossil bones show signs of healing from injuries or disease. This gives us an interesting window into the life of an individual dinosaur. But the daily social habits of dinosaurs left few traces.

Many footprints of dinosaurs have turned to stone, becoming fossilized as trackways. In some cases, the footprints of several dinosaurs together have been found. Some of these prints form long trackways that record a brief moment in time millions of years ago.

Most sauropod trackways that have been found record the movement of more than one animal. One trackway in Texas was left behind by 23 sauropods walking along the shore of an ancient lake. Another trackway in Argentina was made by over 40 sauropods. Evidence like this suggests that *Diplodocus* and other sauropods were herding animals. Living and moving in herds would have offered protection and provided chances for social interaction.

One sauropod trackway shows a sauropod chased by a meat-eating dinosaur. The hunter closes in on its prey, actually stepping into the footprints of the giant dinosaur. The attacker appears to take a hop and sink its teeth into the sauropod. The animal drags its bitten leg and turns left. Then the trackway ends.

A pack of *Allosaurus* tries to get a baby *Diplodocus*. But the herd will use their whip-like tails to keep the predators away.

Some scientists believe that sauropods may have migrated great distances. Animals the size of sauropods would have quickly eaten up local food sources. They may have had to move constantly just to find food.

Fossilized eggs are another kind of evidence that gives us glimpses of a dinosaur's life. Some eggs are found whole, still cradled in their nests. Others are just fossilized fragments of broken shells. Since the embryos inside the eggs rarely fossilize, it is hard to match a specific dinosaur to a specific egg.

We haven't found any nests that we're sure belonged to *Diplodocus*. But scientists have found fossil nests they believe were made by sauropods. They were mounds of soggy leaves and other plant matter, covered with sand or soft earth. The eggs were buried in the center of the mound. Sauropods were too large to sit on nests. The rotting vegetation would have created heat and helped to keep the eggs warm. When the eggs were ready to hatch, the mother sauropod would have dug the hatchlings out. Fossil sauropod eggs are long and oval shaped. The bases are plump, and the eggs taper to a gentle point. The shell resembles that of a modern reptile egg.

The End of an Era

The late Jurassic period was the high point for diplodocids. This was when they reached their largest size and their greatest diversity. By the end of the Jurassic, many species of diplodocids could be found living in all parts of the world.

A predator attacks a diplodocid dinosaur on the shoreline of an ancient river in what is now Texas. This painting is based on a set of fossilized footprints that record the attack.

Diplodocus disappeared from the fossil record about 140 million years ago. So did many of the longer, bigger sauropods. But scientists have learned that the diplodocid family and its close relatives were still going strong at the end of the Age of Dinosaurs. *Nemegtosaurus*, a diplodocid from Mongolia, lived as late as 70 million years ago. It had the familiar long neck and tail of the sauropods.

About 65 million years ago, all dinosaurs became extinct. Almost three-fourths of all living species vanished at that time. Scientists have found evidence that a large asteroid hit the earth at the end of the Age of Dinosaurs. It could have caused worldwide fires that fouled the air and blocked the sun for many, many years. There is also evidence that volcanoes became active at that time. Volcanic ash and smoke may have caused climatic changes that made life difficult for dinosaurs.

We are still not sure why dinosaurs as successful as the sauropods became extinct. Their disappearance may have been hurried along by disease or other changes we don't yet know about. What we know for sure is that 65 million years ago, the giant beasts disappeared forever.

Maiasaura, the "good mother lizard," takes care of her brood of babies. *Diplodocus* may have done the same.

A pair of adult diplodocids amble along in
their never-ending search for food. Sauropods
ate enormous amounts of plant food, and probably left wide paths through the forests as they
traveled and ate. This was important, as the
paths allowed sunlight in to help smaller,
shorter plants to grow. This, in turn, helped to
provide food for the smaller plant-eaters.

GLOSSARY

allosaurs (AL-uh-sawrz): group of meat-eating dinosaurs related to *Allosaurus*.

Allosaurus (AL-uh-SAWR-us): an allosaurid. The most fearsome predator of the Jurassic period.

ankylosaurs (an-KIE-luh-sawrz): group of plant-eating armored dinosaurs with low, barrel-shaped bodies.

Ankylosaurus (an-KIE-luh-SAWR-us): largest of the ankylosaurs. It had an armored head and bony plates.

Apatosaurus (uh-PAT-uh-SAWR-us): a sauropod plant-eater.

Baryonyx (BAR-ee-ON-iks): a meat-eating dinosaur with enormous claws and a crocodile-like head.

brachiosaurids (BRAK-ee-uh-SAWR-idz): cousins of *Diplodocus*. Group of sauropods that were the tallest, heaviest land animals to ever live.

Brachiosaurus (BRAK-ee-uh-SAWR-us): a large sauropod, with longer front legs than hind legs and a giraffe-like stance.

Ceratosaurus (ser-AT-uh-SAWR-us): a meat-eating dinosaur with a horn on its snout.

diplodocids (di-PLOD-uh-sidz): sauropods with longer back legs than front legs and whip-like tails.

Diplodocus (di-PLOD-uh-kus): a sauropod. One of the longest dinosaurs, with a long neck and a long whip-like tail.

extinct (ik-STINKT): no longer existing.

fossil (FAH-sill): a remnant of a living organism that has turned to stone over time.

gastroliths (GAS-tro-liths): stones swallowed by plant-eaters to help break up their food.

gizzards (GIZ-urdz): pockets of the stomach in which food is broken down for digestion.

Maiasaura (MY-uh-SAWR-uh): a hadrosaurid. The name means "good mother lizard."

Mosasaurus (MOH-zah-SAWR-us): a giant meat-eating reptile that lived in the sea.

Nemegtosaurus (neh-MEG-toe-SAWR-us): a plant-eating dinosaur that lived 70 million years ago.

Plesiosaurus (PLEZ-ee-uh-SAWR-us): a long-necked, meat-eating reptile that lived in the sea.

predator (PRED-uh-tor): an animal that hunts and eats other animals for food.

prey (pray): any animal that is hunted as food.

pterosaurs (TERR-uh-sawrz): flying reptiles from the Mesozoic era.

sauropods (SAWR-uh-podz): a group of four-legged, plant-eating dinosaurs.

Sauroposeidon (SORE-oh-pess-EYE-don): a brachiosaurid sauropod; one of the largest animals ever to walk the earth.

Stegosaurus (STEG-uh-SAWR-us): an armor-plated, plant-eating dinosaur.

Supersaurus (soo-per-SAWR-us): a giant brachiosaurid sauropod.

trackways (TRAK-wayz): footprints left in the mud that have changed to stone over a long time.

vertebrae (VER-tuh-bray): the bones that make up an animal's spine.